Level 1 is
some initial
or subjects
number of fi

Special features:

Doctor words

- medicine
- doctor
- ambulance
- emergency
- kit
- stethoscope
- hospital
- patient

Opening pages introduce key subject words

Large, clear labels and captions

Doctor's kit

Doctors have a kit to help patients. The kit has medicine and a stethoscope in it.

I have a stethoscope to help.

- kit
- stethoscope
- medicine

Careful match between text and pictures

Educational Consultant: Geraldine Taylor
Book Banding Consultant: Kate Ruttle
Subject Consultant: Dr Vashti Mason

LADYBIRD BOOKS

UK | USA | Canada | Ireland | Australia
India | New Zealand | South Africa

Ladybird Books is part of the Penguin Random House group of companies whose addresses can be found at global.penguinrandomhouse.com.

www.penguin.co.uk www.puffin.co.uk www.ladybird.co.uk

Penguin Random House UK

First published 2017
003

Copyright © Ladybird Books Ltd, 2017

Printed in China

A CIP catalogue record for this book is available from the British Library

ISBN: 978-0-241-27517-7

All correspondence to
Ladybird Books
Penguin Random House Children's Books
80 Strand, London WC2R 0RL

I am a Doctor

Written by Katie Woolley
Illustrated by John Lund

Contents

Doctor words	8
A doctor's day	10
At the doctor's surgery	12
Doctor's kit	14
In the home	16
Emergency help	18
At the hospital	20
Stay in hospital	22
A BIG emergency!	24

Would you like to be a doctor?	26
Picture glossary	28
Index	30
I am a Doctor quiz	31

Doctor words

medicine

ambulance

doctor

hospital

emergency

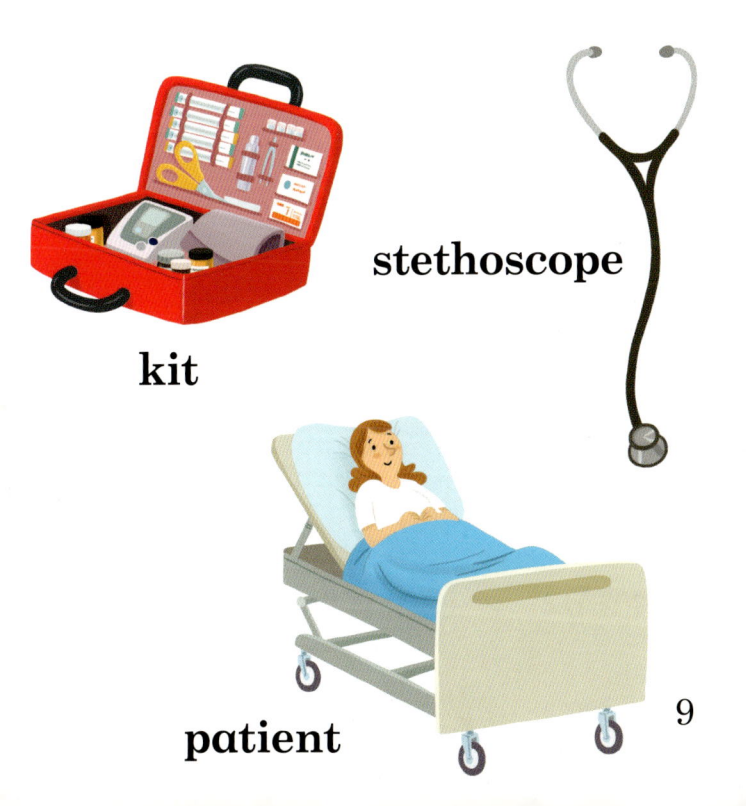

kit

stethoscope

patient

A doctor's day

A doctor helps sick people get better.

Sick people are called patients.

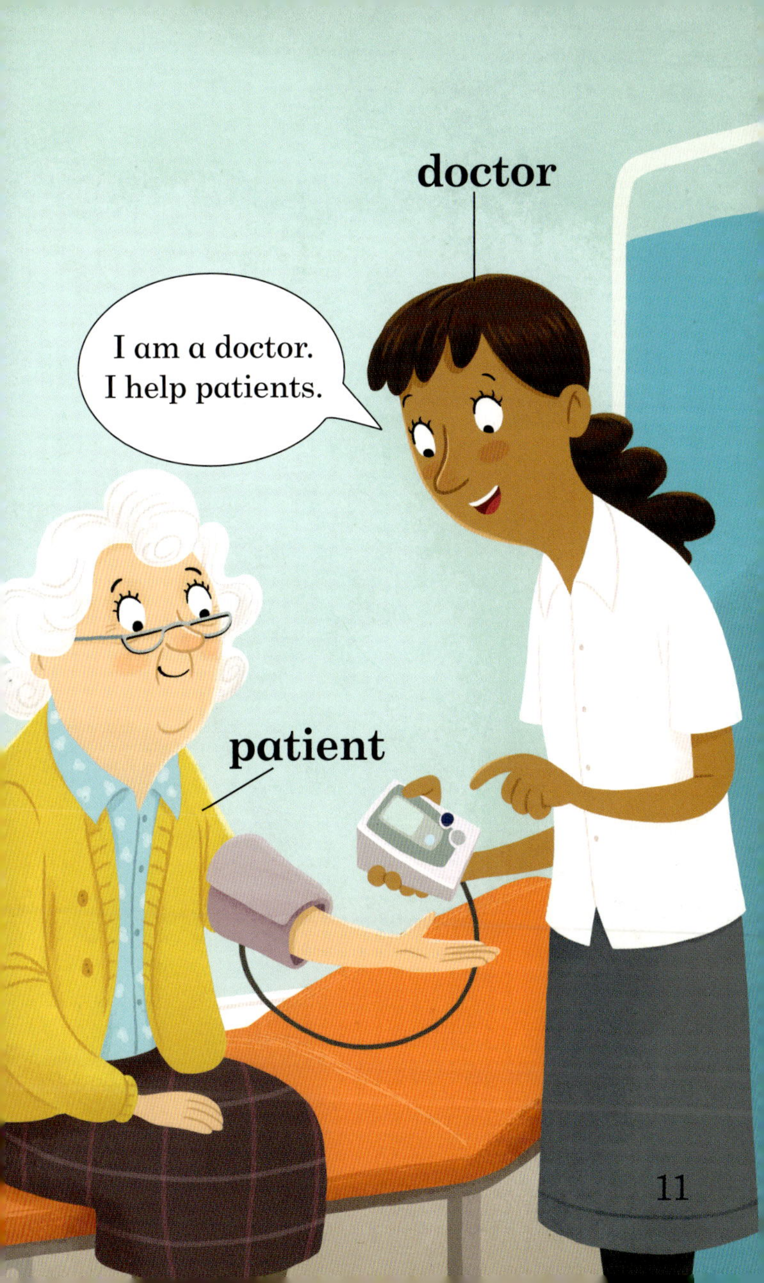
doctor
I am a doctor.
I help patients.
patient

At the doctor's surgery

Patients can see the doctor at the doctor's surgery.

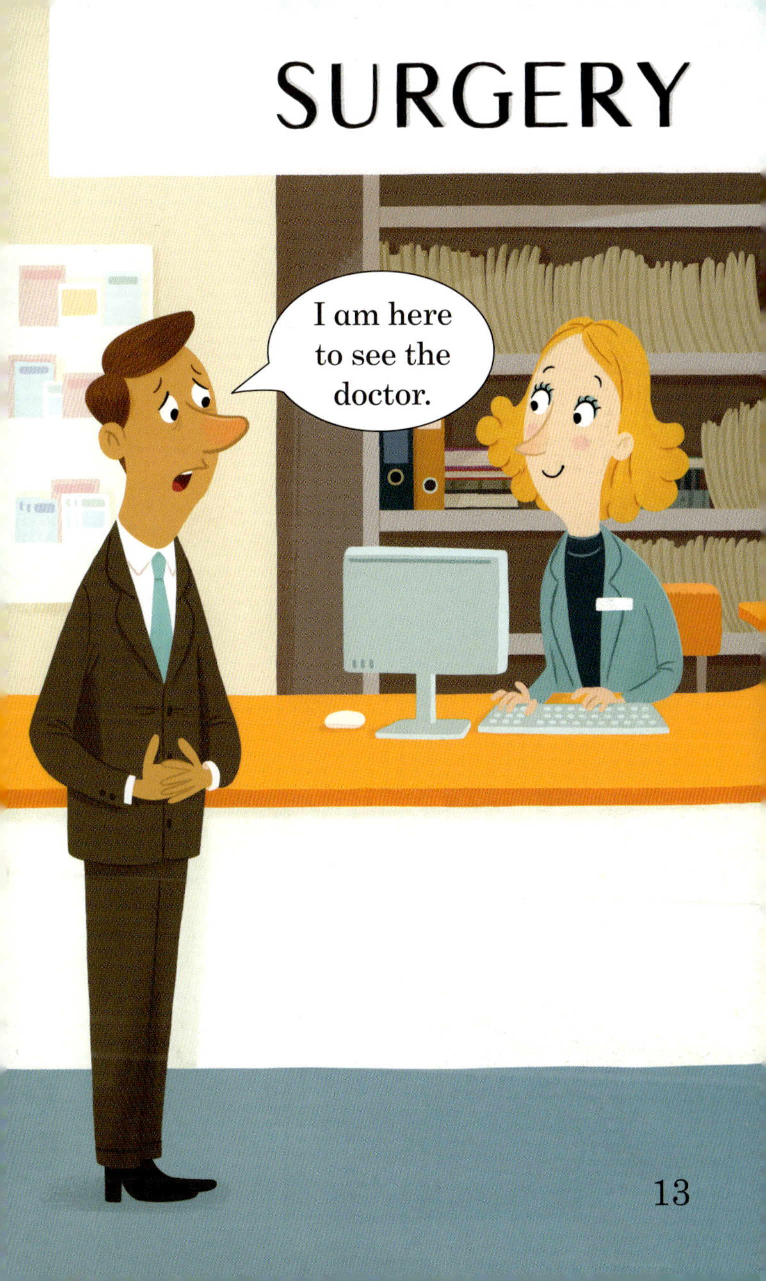
SURGERY
I am here to see the doctor.

Doctor's kit

Doctors have a kit to help patients. The kit has medicine and a stethoscope in it.

I have a stethoscope to help.

kit

medicine

stethoscope

In the home

Doctors can go to see some patients at home, too.

The doctor takes a kit with them that helps people get better.

medicine

kit

Emergency help

An ambulance takes very sick people to hospital to see a doctor. This is called an emergency.

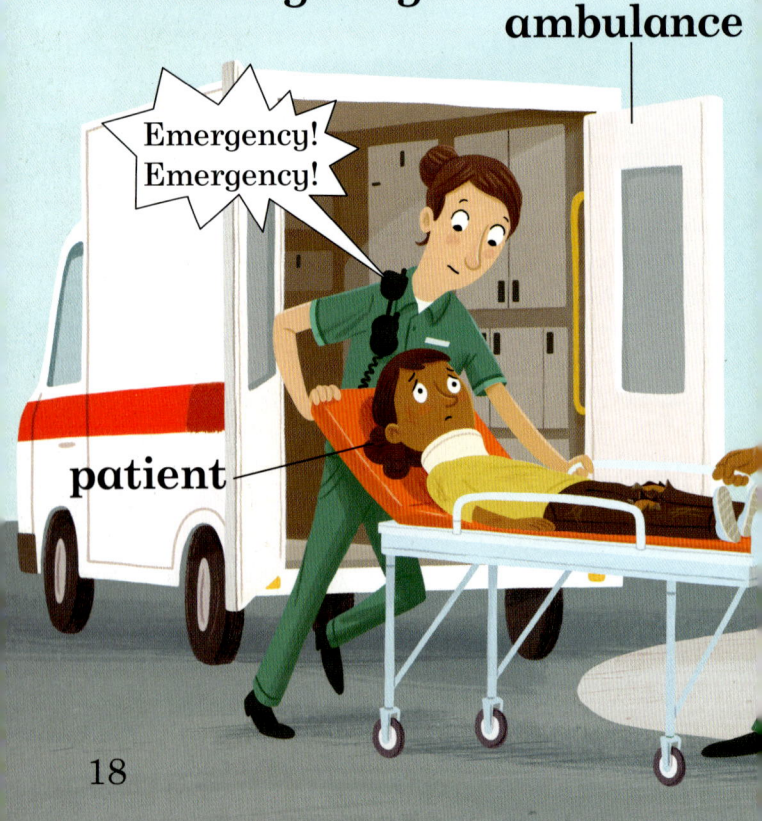

ambulance

patient

Emergency! Emergency!

Accident & Emergency

doctor

At the hospital

At the hospital, doctors look after people who are too sick to be at home.

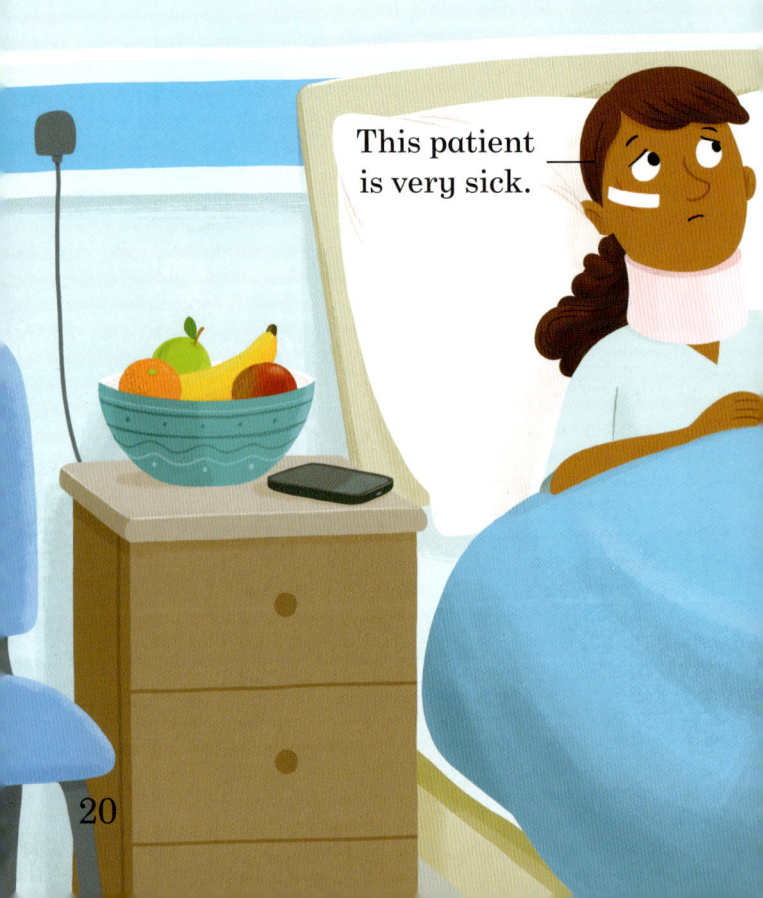

This patient is very sick.

— **doctor**

Stay in hospital

Some patients stay in hospital to get better. A doctor looks after them.

doctor

hospital bed

You are better now. Would you like to go home?

23

A BIG emergency!

Some doctors go to a big emergency.

I am a doctor and I am here to help.

doctor's kit

They take a doctor's kit with them to help.

Would you like to be a doctor?

Doctors help patients get better. They have kits and medicine to help people.

They help at the hospital.

They help at a big emergency.

They help at the surgery.

Would you like to be a doctor one day?

I would like to be a doctor one day.

Picture glossary

ambulance

doctor

emergency

hospital

hospital bed

kit

medicine

patient

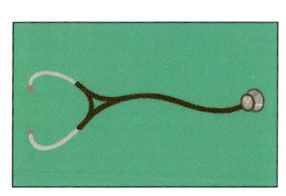

stethoscope

surgery

Index

ambulance	18
emergency	18, 24, 27
hospital	18, 20, 22, 26
hospital bed	23
kit	14, 16, 17, 25
medicine	14, 17
patient	10, 11, 12, 14, 16, 18, 20, 22, 26
stethoscope	14, 15
surgery	12, 13, 27